Hundred and One Verses of Vēmana

Prasanna Vedula Peri

INDIA · SINGAPORE · MALAYSIA

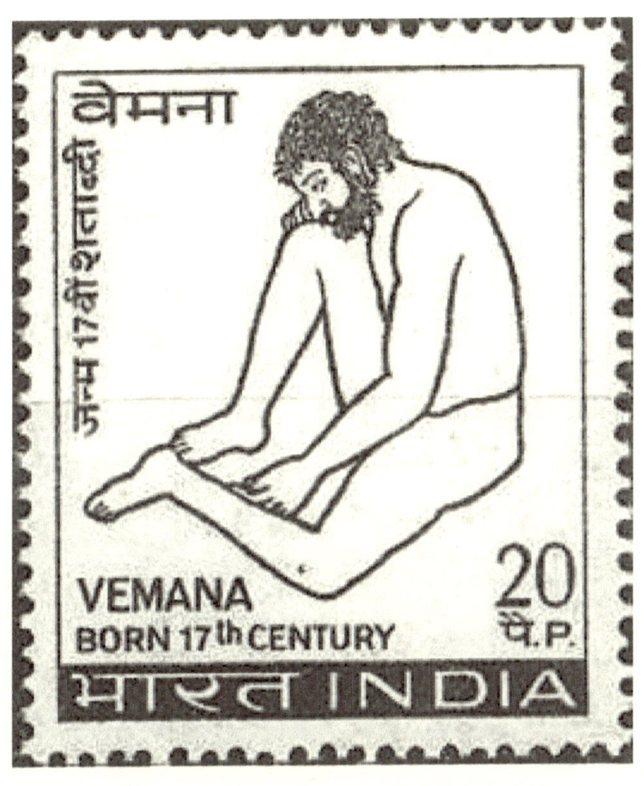

(Commemorative Stamp on Yogi Vēmana,
India Post, 1972)

Dedication

Dedicated to readers like myself – Telugu
speakers who face challenges with its
script but long to immerse themselves in
the beauty of ancient Telugu literature.
I hope these translations transcend
boundaries, illuminate the profound
insights of Mahayogi Vēmana, and inspire
a renewed appreciation for his verses.

Contents

Tribute

To Maha Yogi Vēmana

To Maha Yogi Vēmana, I give my thanks,

With wisdom and wit, you've blessed my soul.

This endeavour is to share your brilliance, beyond the Telugu fold.

Viśvadā-Abhirāma, vinura, Vēma!

Your verses in Telugu, a treasure so bright,

Rhyme and rhythm dance in your light.

My English attempts, mere shadows in the night.

Viśvadā-Abhirāma, vinura, Vēma!

A Journey of Discovery: Author's Note

This endeavour stems from my deep appreciation for ancient Telugu lore and literature. While I have a strong grasp of spoken Telugu, my lack of formal training in reading and writing the language has often left me feeling disconnected from its rich literary heritage. This project is a heartfelt attempt to bridge that gap by capturing and sharing the timeless wisdom and wit of Vēmana's poems with readers across linguistic divides.

The translation project began with enthusiasm but was soon met with formidable challenges. My initial confidence in crafting humorous English poetic lines quickly gave way to the realization that Mahayogi Vēmana's quartets—rooted in ancient dialects and layered meanings—were far more complex than anticipated. Decoding each verse required hours of discussion with Telugu scholars, family members, and mentors to uncover its nuances. Despite these difficulties, the irony, depth, and philosophy within each verse kindled my determination to persist.

Bridging the language barrier was an ongoing struggle. Translating Telugu poetry into English poetry, while retaining its soul, proved to be a daily challenge. Each attempt to recreate the rhythm, beauty, and layered meanings of Vēmana's work tested the limits of both language and creativity.

As many readers may know, Vēmana's works have been studied and translated at various points in history. Notable among these is **C.P. Brown's pioneering translation in 1829,** which contextualized the language and culture of that time and serves as the fountainhead for much of the work that followed. Building on this, scholars such as **Prof. Madhuranthakam Narendra, Dr. Gurram Bhanumurthy** (*Vēmana*, TTD, Tirupati), **A. Meenakshi** (in *Veda's Journal of English Language and Literature*), and resources from institutions like **Maha Yogi Vēmana Peetha** and **Sahitya Akademi** have brought further richness to our understanding. Additionally, online archives such as **TeluguCorner.com, Andhra Bharathi.com, and slokam.in** provided valuable material for exploration and sometimes threw up variations that required further validations with experts. Conversations with friends, Telugu teachers, and fellow enthusiasts also unearthed new perspectives. Despite these extensive resources, I believe this discovery is far from complete, as many more interpretations of Vēmana's works may emerge.

In my view, the gap is in translating Vēmana's Telugu poetry into **poetry in English**, rather than into prose. My endeavour is to preserve the poetic form, conveying Vēmana's rhythm, wit, and profound insights in a contemporary yet faithful English rendition. This task is fraught with difficulty. Telugu's lyrical richness, its cultural idioms, and grammatical nuances like the **Anusvāram rule** ("ka, cha, ta, tha, pa become ga, ja, da, dha, ba") make the process both awe-inspiring and challenging. Vēmana often employed substitutions—using **'ba' instead of 'pa'** or **'ga' instead of 'ka'**—adding layers to his expression that could lead to different meanings. This had to be addressed while maintaining poetic integrity.

One striking example of this complexity is the verse below.

"Pañca mukhamulandu bañcākṣari janiñce / Pañca varṇamulanu prabale jagamu / Pañcamukhuni mīru prastuti cēyuṇḍī"

This verse celebrates the sacred Panchakshari mantra (Om Na Ma Shi Va Ya), tracing its origins to Lord Shiva's five faces and its connection to the five elements and colours. Capturing its profound essence in English was a formidable challenge, yet I approached the translation with humility and deep reverence for Mahayogi Vēmana. My English rendition is included in the book.

For similar poems, post-script commentaries have been included to provide context and address nuances that were especially difficult to convey, compensating for the inevitable subtleties lost in translation.

Similarly, the verse:

"Niṇḍunadulu pāru nilaci gambhīramai / Veṟrivāgu pāṟu vēgaborli / Alpuḍāḍurīti nadhikuṇḍu nāḍunā"

How can the Telugu term "verrivagu" (wild brook) ever truly resonate in English, with its vivid imagery and cultural context? It offers a striking juxtaposition between calm, full rivers and wild, rushing brooks, drawing a metaphor for human character. I attempted to preserve the vivid imagery and the philosophical undertone:

Deep, brimming rivers flow with calm and grandeur,

The wild brook rushes fast and tumultuous.

Would the great behave as the petty do?

Viśvadā-Abhirāma, vinura, Vēma!

Consider this verse - How does one capture the musical beauty of **"Anaga nanaga rāga matiśa yillucunuṇḍu / Dinaga dinaga vēmu tiyyanuṇḍu / Sādhanamuna panulu samakūru dharalōna"**?

In all translations, I chose to retain the signature line, **"Viśvadā-Abhirāma, vinura, Vēma!"**, as a eulogy to Vēmana, a consistent feature of his poetry. Deviations from this form, such as verses ending in only **" Vēma!"**, might represent subsequent interpretations or additions to his original verses. Rather than viewing them as exceptions, I see them in usage (and perhaps modified when the oral form took shape into the many written versions) as a natural progression of Vēmana's thought process, continually challenging societal norms and urging a return to authenticity.

As I delved deeper into translating Vēmana's verses, a compelling parallel emerged: just as Shakespeare's inventive phrases and idioms have become integral to the English language, Vēmana's unique expressions have profoundly influenced Telugu. Both figures have left enduring legacies, shaping cultural norms, offering social commentary, and providing timeless insights into the human experience. What was once unconventional in their works has seamlessly integrated into daily expressions, reflecting the evolving nature of language and thought. Despite shifts in interpretation over time, the core meanings and values in Vēmana's poetry persist, continuing to resonate in our interactions and reflections.

The journey of translating Vēmana has been one of immense discovery and reverence. His words continue to resonate across centuries, offering wisdom, wit, and philosophical depth. My hope is that this work honours his spirit and invites readers to explore the boundless beauty of Telugu literature.

From the vast collection of over 1200 verses attributed to Vēmana, I have chosen these 101. This selection showcases a variety of themes while including some of the most popular and widely recognized verses. They are not arranged in any particular order of importance but are presented as a diverse tapestry of Vēmana's wit, wisdom, and timeless insights.

The Life and Legacy of Yogi Vēmana

Vēmana, a revered poet-saint of the 17th century is celebrated for his profound and enigmatic verses that continue to resonate through the ages. Born in the Kadapa area of Andhra Pradesh, Vēmana's life and works encapsulate a rich tapestry of spirituality, social critique, and philosophical inquiry.

Vēmana's poetry is characterized by its simplicity and depth, often employing a unique style that resonates with the essence of spiritual and existential contemplation. His verses, commonly ending with the refrain "Vishwada-Abhirama, vinura, Vēma!" reflect a poignant narrative of personal transformation and devotion. The recurring mention of Vishwada and Abhirama in his poems is noteworthy and has several interpretations. According to some accounts where these two figures—his beloved and his dear friend, respectively—played crucial roles and suggest his experiences with them may have influenced his shift away from material life. Vēmana's life took a dramatic turn as he chose to embrace asceticism, living a life of simplicity and introspection.

In summary, Vēmana's life and works are a testament to the enduring power of realisation and philosophical inquiry. His poetry not only offers a window into his personal evolution but also provides timeless insights into the human condition. Through his succinct, yet profound verses, Vēmana continues to inspire and challenge readers, inviting them to explore the deeper truths of existence and the essence of true wisdom.

Vēmana's Verses and Haiku: A Comparative Exploration

This collection explores the profound simplicity of Vēmana's poetry and its intriguing parallels with Japanese Haiku. Both Vēmana's verses and Haiku are renowned for their brevity, typically spanning just three lines. They capture deep resonance through concise expression, often juxtaposing contrasting ideas within their limited form.

Haiku, originating in Japan, traditionally consists of three lines following a 5-7-5 syllabic pattern. They encapsulate moments of insight, reflecting on nature, human experiences, or philosophical thoughts, with an emphasis on simplicity, subtlety, and depth.

Similarly, Vēmana's poetry, from the Telugu-speaking region of India, features a comparable structure. His verses are characterized by their brevity and profound meanings, frequently contrasting significant concepts or ideas within a few lines. Known for their wit, humour, and deep moral insights, Vēmana's poems resonate with the Haiku's focus on capturing the essence of a moment or thought in a few words.

Additionally, many of his poems follow the **Chaatu Padyam** style. This literary device deploys a light-hearted and delightful form of poetry embellished with wit and brevity and often carries implicit meaning.

Vēmana's poetry beautifully follows the Aataveladi style, a metrical form in Telugu literature often likened to a "dancing damsel" for its lyrical grace and captivating rhythm. Each verse flows melodiously, enhancing its philosophical depth while making it accessible and memorable to listeners. The rhythmic elegance of Aataveladi, combined with Vēmana's wit and wisdom, brings his timeless messages vividly to life.

In translating and presenting Vēmana's verses, this collection aims to highlight the shared characteristics of brevity, depth, and juxtaposition that define both poetic forms. This exploration not only celebrates the timeless quality of Vēmana's work but also invites readers to appreciate the universal elements connecting diverse poetic traditions across cultures.

SECTION 1

MORALS FROM
THE ANIMAL REALM

1

గంగిగోవుపాలు గరిటెడైననను జాలు

కడివెడైననేమి ఖరముపాలు

భక్తిగలుగుకూడు పట్టెడైననను జాలు

విశ్వదాభిరామ వినుర వేమ!

Gaṅgigōvupālu gariṭeḍainanu jālu

kaḍiveḍainanēmi kharamupālu

bhaktigalugukūḍu paṭṭeḍainanu jālu

viśvadābhirāma vinura vēma.

From the gentle cow, a ladleful of milk
suffices;

What worth is a potful from a donkey?

For when offered with love, even a mere
handful satiates.

Viśvadā-Abhirāma, vinura, Vēma!

2

ఎలుగు తోలు తెచ్చి ఏడాది యుతికినా

నలుపు నలుపేకాని తెలుపుకాదు

కొయ్యబొమ్మ తెచ్చి కొట్టితే గుణియోనె

విశ్వదాభిరామ వినుర వేమ!

Elugu tōlu tecci ēḍādi yutikinā

Nalupu nalupēkāni telupukādu

Koyyabom'ma tecci koṭṭitē guṇiyōne

Viśvadābhirāma vinura, Vēma!

Wash a bear's hide through the year with utmost care,

Yet black as ebony, it remains—no whitening to declare.

Thrash a wooden doll as you may, no song will it bear.

Viśvadā-Abhirāma, vinura, Vēma!

Hundred and One Verses of Vēmana   28

3

చెప్పులోని రాయి చెవిలోని జోరీగ

కంటిలోని నలుసు కాలి ముల్లు

ఇంటిలోని పోరు నింతింత గాదయా

విశ్వదాభిరామ వినుర వేమ!

Ceppulōni rāyi cevilōni jōrīga

Kaṇṭilōni nalusu kāli mullu

Iṇṭilōni pōru nintinta gādayā

Viśvadābhirāma vinura, Vēma!

A pebble in your shoe, a bee's buzz near
your ear,

A speck in your eye, a thorn in your foot—

A quarrel at home is no trivial annoyance.

Viśvadā-Abhirāma, vinura, Vēma!

4

నీళ్ళలోన మొసలి నిగిడి యెనుంగు బట్టు

బయట కుక్కచేత భంగపడును

స్థానబలముగాని తన బలిమికాదయా

విశ్వదాభిరామ వినురవేమ!

Nīḷḷalōna mosali nigiḍi yenuṅgu baṭṭu

Bayaṭa kukkacēta bhaṅgapaḍunu

Sthānabalamugāni tana balimikādayā

Viśvadābhirāma vinura, Vēma!

In water, a crocodile seizes an elephant,
with might,

On the road, a dog's bark, an insult takes
flight.

'Tis the power of the place, not their own.

Viśvadā-Abhirāma, vinura, Vēma!

5

ము్చ్చ గుడికి పోయి ముడివిప్పునే కాని

పొసగ స్వామిజూచి మ్రొక్కడతడు

కుక్క యిల్లుసొచ్చి కుండలు వెదుకదా

విశ్వదాభిరామ! వినుర వేమ!

Mruccu guḍiki pōyi muḍivippunē kāni

Posaga svāmijūci mrokkaḍataḍu

Kukka yillusocci kuṇḍalu vedukadā

Viśvadābhirāma! Vinura, Vēma!

Into the temple, a thief sneaks, with theft in mind,

Seeing the divine, no prayer does he find.

Does a dog not enter a home, seeking only food?

Viśvadā-Abhirāma, vinura, Vēma!

6

పాల నీటి కలత పరమహంస మెఱుగును

నీరు పాలు నెట్లు నేర్చునెమలి

లజ్జుడైన హీనుడల శివు నెఱుగునా?

విశ్వదాభిరామ వినుర వేమ!

Pāla nīṭi kalata paramahansa meṟugunu
Nīru pālu neṭlu nērcunemali
Lajñuḍaina hīnuḍala śivu neṟugunā?
Viśvadābhirāma vinura, vēma!

The great swan discerns the blend of milk
from water,
How can a peacock separate milk from
water?
How can the ignorant and shameless ever
know Shiva?
Viśvadā-Abhirāma, vinura, Vēma!

 The *hamsa* or swan is often associated with the ability to separate milk from water, symbolizing the capacity to distinguish truth from falsehood or essence from the superficial. By using *paramahamsa,* Vēmana elevates this metaphor to represent a spiritually enlightened being who discerns the ultimate truth.

7

పసుల వన్నె వేరు పాలెల్ల ఒక్కటి

పుష్పజాతి వేరు పూజ ఒకటి

దర్శనంటులారు దైవంటు ఒక్కటి

విశ్వదాభిరామ వినుర వేమ!

Pasula vanne vēru pālella okkaṭi

Puṣpajāti vēru pūja okaṭi

Darśanambulāru daivambu okkaṭi

Viśvadābhirāma vinura vēma!

Animals' colours may differ, yet their milk is
the same,

Flowers come in many hues, but the prayer
is the same,

Philosophies are Six, yet the divine is One.

Viśvadā-Abhirāma, vinura, Vēma!

The term *darsanam* also refers to any one of the six traditional schools of Hindu philosophy and their literature on spirituality and soteriology (the study of religious doctrines of salvation).

They are:

1. *Samkhya* is the earliest school of dualism

2. *Yoga* combines the metaphysics of Samkhya with meditation and breath techniques;

3. *Nyaya* is a school of logic emphasising direct realism;

4. *Vaisheshika* is an offshoot of *Nyaya* concerned with atomism and naturalism;

5. *Mimamsa* is a school justifying ritual, faith, and religious obligations; and

6. *Vedanta* contains various traditions that mostly embrace nondualism.

8

మేక కుతుక బట్టి మెడచన్ను గడువుగా

ఆకలేల మాను నాశగాక

లోభివాని నడుగ లాభంబు లేదయా

విశ్వదాభిరామ వినురవేమ!

Mēka kutuka baṭṭi meḍacannu gaḍuvugā

Akalēla mānu nāśagāka

Lōbhivāni naḍuga lābhambu lēdayā

Viśvadābhirāma vinuravēma!

Grasping the goat's throat, drawing from its neck glands—

How can it truly satisfy hunger? The yearning remains.

There's no gain in seeking from a miser.

Viśvadā-Abhirāma, vinura, Vēma!

9

అల్పబుద్ధివానికధికారమిచ్చిన
దొడ్డవారినెల్ల తొలగగొట్టు
చెప్పుదినెడు కుక్క చెరకు తీపెరుగునా
విశ్వదాభిరామ వినుర వేమ!

Alpabud'dhivānikadhikāramiccina

Doḍḍavārinella tolagagoṭṭu

Ceppudineḍu kukka ceraku tīperugunā

Viśvadābhirāma vinura, Vēma!

By elevating the less intelligent,

You diminish the superior.

Does a slipper-chewing dog savour
sugarcane's sweetness?

Viśvadā-Abhirāma, vinura, Vēma!

10

ఆలిమాటలు విని అన్నదమ్ముల రోసి
వేరేపోవువాడు వెర్రివాడు
కుక్కతోక పట్టి గోదారీదినా?
విశ్వదాభిరామ వినుర వేమ!

Ālimāṭalu vini annadam'mula rōsi
Vērēpōvuvāḍu verrivāḍu
Kukkatōka paṭṭi gōdārīdinā?
Viśvadābhirāma vinura, vēma!

He who heeds his wife but neglects his
brothers,
Straying far from his kin, proves himself a
fool.
Can one cross the Godavari by clinging to a
dog's tail?
Viśvadā-Abhirāma, vinura, Vēma!

The poem highlights the folly of relying on trivial or unsuitable means, such as clinging to a dog's tail, to cross the mighty Godavari river. It serves as a metaphor for the importance of wisdom and discernment when navigating life's significant undertakings.

11

ఆశచేత మనుజ లాయువు గలనాళ్ళు

తిరుగుచుంద్రు భ్రమను ద్రిప్పలేక

మురికికుండమందు ముసురునీగల భంగి

విశ్వదాభిరామ వినురవేమ!

Āśacēta manuju lāyuvu galanāḷḷu

Tirugu cuṇḍru bhramanu drippalēka

Murikikuṇḍamandu musurunīgala bhaṅgi

Viśvadābhirāma vinura, vēma!

People cling to the hope of eternal life,

Going in circles, in an illusion they can't
break,

Like flies swarming over a murky pond.

Viśvadā-Abhirāma, vinura, Vēma!

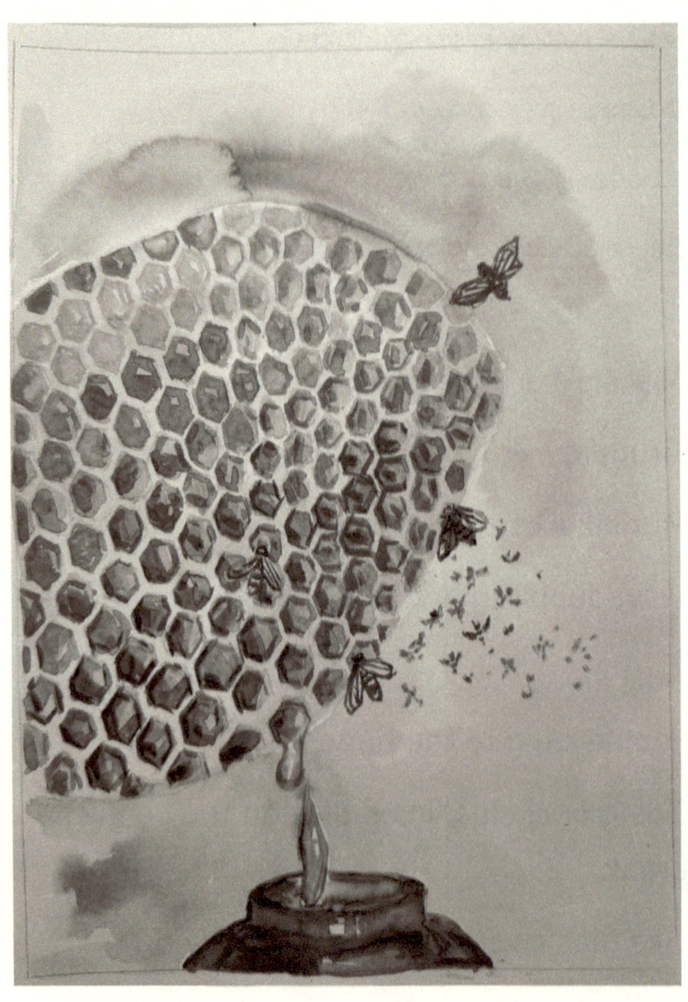

12

ధనము గూడబెట్టి దానంటు చేయక

తానుందినక లెస్స దాచుకొనగ

తేనెటీగ కూర్చి తెరువరి కియ్యదా

విశ్వదాభిరామ వినురవేమ!

Dhanamu gūḍabeṭṭi dānambu cēyaka

Tānundinaka les'sa dācukonaga

Tēneṭīga kūrci teruvari kiyyadā

Viśvadābhirāma vinuravēma!

Amassing wealth, yet withholding aid,

Not enjoying, but hoarding lots.

Does the bee not craft honey, only to share with others?

Viśvadā-Abhirāma, vinura, Vēma!

13

పాలపిట్ట శకున ఫలమిచ్చునందురు
పాలపిట్ట కేమి ఫలము తెలియు
తనదు మేలుకీళ్ళు తనతోడనుండగ
విశ్వదాభిరామ వినురవేమ!

Pālapiṭṭa śakuna phalamiccunanduru
pālapiṭṭa kēmi phalamu teliyu
tanadu mēlukīḷḷu tanatōḍanuṇḍaga
Viśvadābhirāma vinuravēma!

The Paalapitta bird brings a sign, an omen bright,
Yet what can it reveal of wrong or right?
Isn't the power to shape one's fate in one's own hands?
Viśvadā-Abhirāma, vinura, Vēma!

Paalapitta, known as the Indian Roller is the state bird of the Indian states of Odisha, Telangana, and Karnataka. It is noted for its distinctive call and is often associated with certain folklore and cultural references in Indian languages.

14

పరులమేలు చూసి పలుకాకి వలె

వట్టిమాటలాడు వాడు అధముడు

అట్టివాని బతుకుటది ఏల మంటికా?

విశ్వదాభిరామ వినుర వేమ!

Parulamēlu chūsi palukāki vale

Vaṭṭimāṭalāḍu vāḍu adhamuḍu

Aṭṭivāni batukuṭadi ēla maṇṭikā?

Viśvadābhirāma Vinura, Vēma!

The one who, like a crow, squawks and speaks ill,

Scorning the good that others fulfill, is but a wasted soul.

What purpose does such a life hold? To fade into dust?

Viśvadā-Abhirāma, vinura, Vēma!

చిక్కియున్నవేళ సింహంబునైనను

బక్క కుక్కయైన బాధసేయు

బలిమిలేని వేళ పంతములు చెల్లవు

విశ్వదాభిరామ వినుర వేమ!

Cikkiyunnavēḷa sinhambunainanu

Bakka kukkayaina bādhasēyu

Balimilēni vēḷa pantamulu cellavu

Viśvadābhirāma vinura vēma!

Even a lion, when weak,

Can be troubled by a mere bony dog.

In weakness, obstinacy will not succeed.

Viśvadā-Abhirāma, vinura, Vēma!

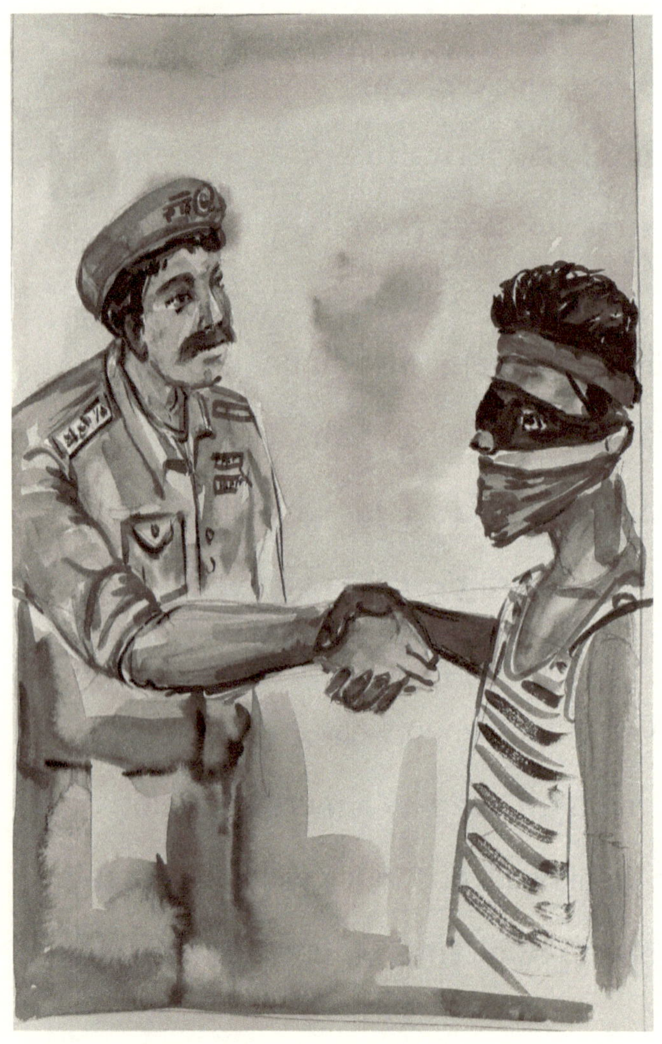

Hundred and One Verses of Vēmana   54

16

కొండముచ్చు పెండ్లికి కోతి పేరంటాలు

మొండి వాని హితుడు బండవాడు

దుండగీడునకును కొండెడు దళవాయి

విశ్వదాభిరామా వినుర వేమ!

Koṇḍamuccu peṇḍliki kōti pēraṇṭālu

Moṇḍi vāni hituḍu baṇḍavāḍu

Duṇḍagīḍunakunu koṇḍeḍu daḷavāyi

Viśvadābhirāmā vinura vēma!

The monkey is the guest at the langur's wedding,

The fool acts as the well-wisher for the stubborn one,

And the lawkeeper serves as the arbiter for the thug.

Viśvadā-Abhirāma, vinura, Vēma!

ఝుషము నీరు వెడల జచ్చుటే సిద్ధము

నీటనుండనేని నిక్కిపడును

అండతొలుగు నెడల నందర పని అట్లే

విశ్వదాభి రామ వినుర వేమ!

Jhuṣamu nīru veḍala jaccuṭē sid›dhamu

Nīṭanuṇḍanēni nikkipaḍunu

Aṇḍatolugu neḍala nandara pani aṭlē

Viśvadābhi rāma vinura Vēma!

If a fish leaves the water, death is certain,

But within the water, it flourishes and lives.

Without support, we too are bound to perish.

Viśvadā-Abhirāma, vinura, Vēma!

18

మేక జంకటెట్టిమెలగుచు మందలో

బ్రమని తిరుగు గొల్ల పగిదిగాను

దేవునెరుగక పరదపేతల దలచు

విశ్వదాభిరామ వినుర వేమ!

Mēka jaṅkabeṭṭimelaguchu mandalō

Bramani tirugu golla pagidigānu

Dēvunerugaka paradavētala dalachu

Viśvadābhirāma Vinura, Vēma!

Carrying a goat under your arm, lost among the herd,

Wandering like a shepherd, adrift in thought,

Failing to grasp the divine, you brood over your own troubles.

Viśvadā-Abhirāma, vinura, Vēma!

19

ఐకమత్యమొక్క టావశ్యకం బెప్పు

దాని బలిమి నెంతయైన గూడు

గడ్డి వెంట బెట్టి కట్టరా యేనుంగు

విశ్వదాభిరామ వినుర వేమ!

Aikamatyamokka ṭāvaśyakaṁ bepḍu

Dāni balimi nentayaina gūḍu

Gaḍḍi veṇṭa beṭṭi kaṭṭarā yēnuṅgu

Viśvadābhirāma vinura vēma!

Unity is essential at all times,

For with its strength, great feats are achieved.

Do we not bind an elephant with a rope of straw?

Viśvadā-Abhirāma, vinura, Vēma!

SECTION 2

NATURE AND PLANTS

20

అనువుగాని చోట నధికుల మనరాదు.

కొంచముండు టెల్ల గొదువగాదు

కొండ యద్దమందు గొంచెమైయ్యుండదా!

విశ్వదాభిరామ వినురవేమ!!

Anuvugāni cōṭa nadhikula manarādu.

Koñcamuṇḍu ṭella goduvagādu

Koṇḍa yaddamandu goñcemaiyuṇḍadā!

Viśvadābhirāma vinura,Vēma!!

Where conditions oppose, shun superiority's claim,

For humility brings no loss, nor does it diminish worth.

Does the grand, towering mountain not shrink in the mirror's view?

Viśvadā-Abhirāma, vinura, Vēma!

21

చిప్పబడ్డ స్వాతిచినుకు ముత్యంబాయె

నీటిబడ్డ చినుకు నీటగలిసె

బ్రాప్తికలుగుచోట ఫలమేల తప్పురా

విశ్వదాభిరామ వినురవేమ!

Cippabaḍḍa svāticinuku mutyambāye

Nīṭibaḍḍa cinuku nīṭagalise

Brāptikalugucōṭa phalamēla tappurā

Viśvadābhirāma vinura, Vēma!

In an oyster's embrace, a drop of water transforms into a pearl divine,

Whilst in a vast ocean, it simply blends, disappears.

Likewise, in an opportune place, blessings and success flow, undeniably!

Viśvadā-Abhirāma, vinura, Vēma!

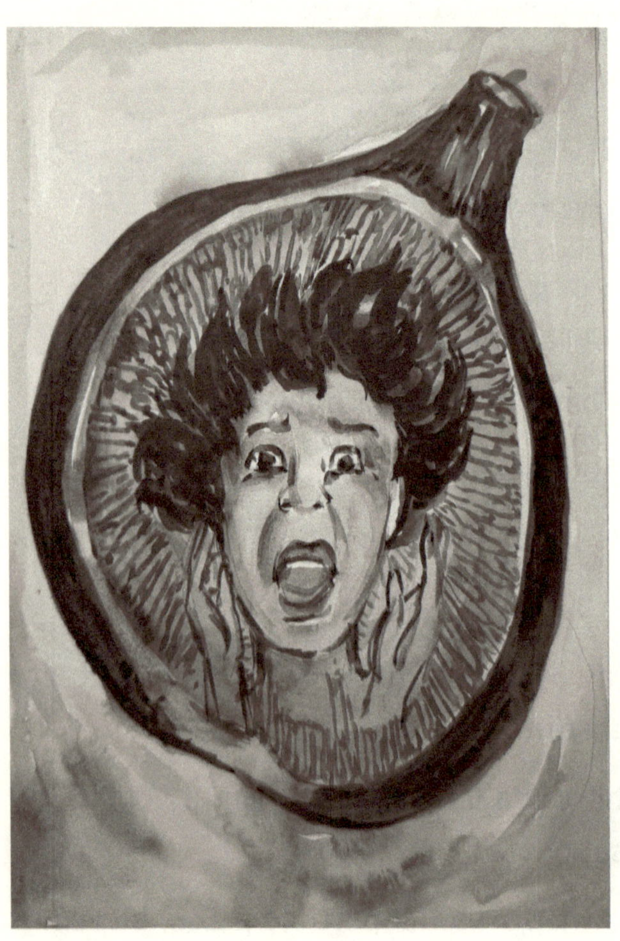

22

మేడిపండుచూడ మేలిమై యుండు

పొట్టవిప్పిచూడంటురుగులుుండు

పిరికివాని మదిని బింకమీలాగురా

విశ్వదాభిరామ వినురవేమ!

Mēḍipaṇḍucūḍa mēlimai yuṇḍu

Poṭṭavippicūḍamburuguluṇḍu

Pirikivāni madini biṅkamīlāgurā

Viśvadābhirāma vinura,Vēma!

A fig may allure with its exterior gleam,

But within, worms lurk, unseen.

Thus, deep within a coward, fear's extreme!

Viśvadā-Abhirāma, vinura, Vēma!

23

మిరపగింజచూడ మీద నల్లగనుండం

గొరికిచూడ లోన జరుకు మనును

సజ్జనులగువారి సారమిట్లుండరా!

విశ్వదాభిరామ వినురవేమ!

Mirapagiñjacūḍa mīda nallaganuṇḍum

Gorikicūḍa lōna juruku manunu

Sajjanulaguvāri sāramiṭluṇḍarā!

Viśvadābhirāma vinura,Vēma!

A black peppercorn may seem puny

But bite into it, fiery hot!

So are the wise - humble, yet potent.

Viśvadā-Abhirāma, vinura, Vēma!

24

అలను బుగ్గ పుట్టినప్పుడే క్షయమౌను
కలనుం గాంచులక్ష్మి కల్లయగును
ఇలను భోగభాగ్య మీతిరు కాదొకో
విశ్వదాభిరామ వినురవేమ!

Alanu bugga puṭṭinappuḍē kṣayamaunu
Kalanuṁ gāñculakṣmi kallayagunu
Ilanu bhōgabhāgya mītīru kādokō
Viśvadābhirāma vinura,vēma!

The bubble on a wave bursts as it forms,
The riches seen in a dream fade upon waking.
Are not our worldly pleasures, indulgences, and fortunes the same?
Viśvadā-Abhirāma, vinura, Vēma!

While some interpret *alanu bugga* as fire in the ocean (a rare phenomenon of fire within the ocean that vanishes instantly), my instinct leaned toward *bugga* (short of *budaga*) as a bubble on the wave. In this verse, I felt bubble was more relatable and aligned in the context of an ocean.

25

పరగ ఊతిగుండు బగులగొట్టగ వచ్చు

గొండలన్ని పిండి గొట్టవచ్చు

కఠిన చిత్తు మనసు కరిగింపరాదు

విశ్వదాభిరామ వినురవేమ!

Paraga r̄ātiguṇḍu bagulagoṭṭaga vaccu

Goṇḍalanni piṇḍi goṭṭavaccu

Kaṭhina cittu manasu karigimparādu

Viśvadābhirāma vinura,Vēma!

Strive as much,

Hard rocks may be shattered, mountains crumbled to dust,

But a hard, mean heart cannot be melted.

Viśvadā-Abhirāma, vinura, Vēma!

26

అనగ ననగ రాగ మతిశ యిల్లుచునుణ్డు

దినగ దినగ వేము తియ్యనుణ్డు

సాధనమున పనులు సమకూరు ధరలోన

విశ్వదాభిరామ వినుర వేమ!

Anaga nanaga rāga matiśa yillucunuṇḍu

Dinaga dinaga vēmu tiyyanuṇḍu

Sādhanamuna panulu samakūru dharalōna

Viśvadābhirāma vinura, Vēma!

Sung repeatedly, melodies linger sweet and strong,

With each bite, Neem's bitterness soon sweetens along.

Through practice, tasks become easy, swift, and thorough.

Viśvadā-Abhirāma, vinura, Vēma!

27

ముష్టి వేపచెట్టు మొదలంట ప్రజలకు

బరగ మూలికలకు బనికివచ్చు

నిర్దయాత్మకుండు నీచుడెందులకౌను

విశ్వదాభిరామ వినురవేమ!

Muṣṭi vēpaceṭṭu modalaṇṭa prajalaku

Baraga mūlikalaku banikivaccu

Nirdayātmakuṇḍu nīcuḍendulakaunu

Viśvadābhirāma vinuravēma!

Even the roots of the bitterest Neem tree
Find purpose as healing herbal medicine.
But what worth is there for the cruel and
ruthless?
Viśvadā-Abhirāma, vinura, Vēma!

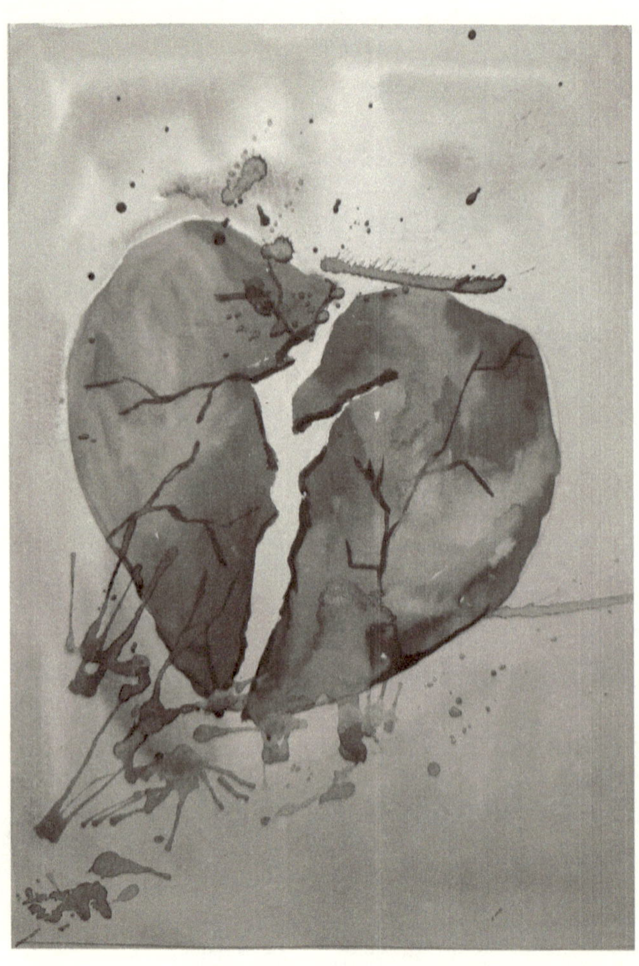

28

ఇనుము విరిగెనేని యినుమారు ముమ్మారు

కాల్చి యతుకవచ్చు క్రమముగాను

మనసు విరిగెనేని మరికూర్ప వచ్చునా

విశ్వదాభిరామ వినురవేమ!

Inumu virigenēni yinumāru mum'māru

Kālci yatukavaccu kramamugānu

Manasu virigenēni marikūrpa vaccunā

Viśvadābhirāma vinura, Vēma!

Iron, broken once or even many times,

Can be forged anew with heat, restored to its form.

But can a broken heart ever be whole again?

Viśvadā-Abhirāma, vinura, Vēma!

నిండునదులు పారు నిలచి గంభీరమై

వెఱ్ఱివాగు పాఱు వేగబొర్లి

అల్పుడాడురీతి నధికుండు నాడునా

విశ్వదాభిరామ వినుర వేమ!

Niṇḍunadulu pāru nilaci gambhīramai

Veṟrivāgu pāṟu vēgaborli

Alpuḍāḍurīti nadhikuṇḍu nāḍunā

Viśvadābhirāma vinura vēma!

Deep, brimming rivers flow with calm and grandeur,

The wild brook rushes fast and tumultuous,

Would the great behave as the petty do?

Viśvadā-Abhirāma, vinura, Vēma!

భూమిలోన బుట్టు భూసారమెల్లను

తనువులోన బుట్టు తత్త్వమెల్ల

శ్రమలోన బుట్టు సర్వంబు తానౌను

విశ్వదాభిరామ వినుర వేమ!

Bhūmilōna buṭṭu bhūsāramellanu

Tanuvulōna buṭṭu tattvamella

Sramalōna buṭṭu sarvambu tānaunu

Viśvadābhirāma vinura, Vēma!

All fruitfulness of the Earth is born within the Earth

All attributes are born within our body

Everything born from your labour becomes YOU.

Viśvadā-Abhirāma, vinura, Vēma!

31

ఎండిన మానొకటడవిని

మండిన నందగ్ని పుట్టి యూడ్చును చెట్లన

దండిగల వంశమెల్లను

చండాలుండొకడు పుట్టి చదువును వేమ!

Eṇḍina mānokaṭaḍavini

Maṇḍina nandagni puṭṭi yūḍcunu ceṭlan

Daṇḍigala vanśamellanu

Caṇḍāluṇḍokaḍu puṭṭi caduvunu vēma!

Even a single dry tree, if ignited,

Can set ablaze all that surrounds.

One vile child born in the family

Can ruin an entire esteemed lineage, Vēma!

32

తుమ్మచెట్టు ముండ్ల తోడనేపుట్టును

విత్తులోననుండు వెడలునట్లు

మూర్ఖునకును బుద్ధి ముందుగా బుట్టను

విశ్వదాభిరామ వినుర వేమ!

Tum'macettu muṇḍla tōḍanēputtunu

Vittulōnanuṇḍu veḍalunaṭlu

Mūrkhunakunu bud'dhi mundugā buttanu

Viśvadābhirāma vinura, Vēma!

The Acacia tree is born with thorns,

Its seed preserves its nature,

A fool's foolishness, too, is sown from the start.

Viśvadā-Abhirāma, vinura, Vēma!

వేరు పురుగు చేరి వృక్షంబు జెరుచును

చీడపురుగు చేరి చెట్టు జెరచు

కుత్సితుండు చేరి గుణవంతు జెరచురా

విశ్వదాభిరామ వినుర వేమ!

Vēru purugu cēri vr̥kṣambu jerucunu

Cīḍapurugu cēri ceṭṭu jeracu

Kutsituṇḍu cēri guṇavantu jeracurā

Viśvadābhirāma vinura vēma!

Root rot infects and destroys the tree,

Termites invade and ruin the woods.

A wicked one joins the virtuous, only to
bring about their ruin.

Viśvadā-Abhirāma, vinura, Vēma!

SECTION 3

ON DIVINITY

34

తలపులోన గలుగు దా దైవమే ప్రొద్దు

తలచి చూడనటకు తత్త్వమగును

వూఱకుణ్ణ నేర్వనుత్తమ యోగిరా

విశ్వదాభిరామ వినుర వేమ!

Talapulōna galugu dā daivamē proddu

Talaci cūḍanataku tattvamagunu

Vūṟakuṇḍa nērvunuttama yōgirā

Viśvadābhirāma vinura, Vēma!

Doesn't dawn emerge as divine?

Contemplate, for therein the true essence shines.

He who knows this, without learning, is truly enlightened.

Viśvadā-Abhirāma, vinura, Vēma!

35

ఆత్మ శుద్ధిలేని ఆచార మధియేలా

భాండ శుద్ధి లేని పాకమేల

చిత్తశుద్ధి లేని శివపూజయేలరా

విశ్వదాభిరామ వినుర వేమ!

Ātmaśuddilēni ācāra madhiyēlā

Bhāṇḍa śud'dhi lēni pākamēla

Cittaśud'dhi lēni śivapūjayēlarā

Viśvadābhirāma vinura, Vēma!

Of what use are rites and rituals when the
soul is tarnished,

Of what use is the sweet when cooked in a
vessel unclean,

Of what use are prayers when the
conscience is tainted?

Viśvadā-Abhirāma, vinura, Vēma!

తపముపేల? యరయ ధాత్రిజనులకెల్ల

నొనర శివుని జూడ నుపమ గలదు

మనసు చదరనీక మహిలోన జూడరా

విశ్వదాభిరామ వినుర పేమ!

Tapamuvēla? Yaraya dhātrijanulakella

Nonara śivuni jūḍa nupama galadu

Manasu cadaranīka mahilōna jūḍarā

Viśvadābhirāma vinura, vēma!

Why meditate, O people of the world?

Steady your mind, seek Shiva, and find his protection.

Only ensure the mind stays calm and undisturbed while walking this Earth.

Viśvadā-Abhirāma, vinura, Vēma!

37

వెన్న చేతబట్టి వివరంబు తెలియక
ఘృతము కోరునట్టి యతని భండి
తాను దైవమయ్యు దైవంబు దలచును
విశ్వదాభిరామ వినుర వేమ!

Venna cētabaṭṭi vivarambu teliyaka
Ghṛtamu kōrunaṭṭi yatani bhaṇḍi
Tānu daivamayyu daivambu dalacunu
Viśvadābhirāma vinura, Vēma!

Holding butter in his hand, unaware of its worth,
He seeks ghee—that defines his nature.
He is God Himself, yet searches for God.
Viśvadā-Abhirāma, vinura, Vēma!

38

పంచ ముఖములందు బంచాక్షరి జనించె

పంచ వర్ణములను ప్రబలె జగము

పంచముఖుని మీరు ప్రస్తుతి చేయుండి

విశ్వదాభిరామ వినుర వేమ!

Pañca mukhamulandu bañcākṣari janiñce
Pañca varṇamulanu prabale jagamu
Pañcamukhuni mīru prastuti cēyuṇḍī
Viśvadābhirāma vinura, vēma!

The five syllables emerged from the five-
faced Shiva;
The five colours owe their existence to him;
Pray to him with devotion.
Viśvadā-Abhirāma, vinura, Vēma!

The Five Syllables- Om Na Mah Shi Vay

The Five Colours-Red, Green, Yellow, Black, and White

వ్రాతకంటె హెచ్చు పరమీదు దైవంటు
చేతకంటె హెచ్చు వ్రాత లేదు
వ్రాత కజుడు కర్త చేతకు దాకర్త
విశ్వదాభిరామ వినుర వేమ!

Vrātakaṇṭe heccu paramīdu daivambu
Cētakaṇṭe heccu vrāta lēdu
Vrāta kajuḍu karta cētaku dākarta
Viśvadābhirāma vinura vēma!

The Almighty grants no more than what's
destined,
No fate exceeds the scope of our actions.
Brahma may govern destiny, but our deeds
are ours alone.
Viśvadā-Abhirāma, vinura, Vēma!

Brahma, the Creator in the Hindu pantheon, symbolizes the essence of creation and the origin of all beginnings. As the divine author of destiny, he is believed to write the fate of every being.

6
1
2
8
9
6
7

40

తనదు మనసుచేత దర్కించి జ్యోతిష
మెంత చేసే ననుచు నెంచి చూచు,
తన యదృష్టమంత దైవ మెఱుంగడా?
విశ్వదాభిరామ వినుర వేమ!

Tanadu manasucēta darkiñci jyōtiṣa
Menta cēsē nanucu neñci cūcu,
Tana yadṛṣṭamanta daiva meṟuṅgaḍā?
Viśvadābhirāma vinura, Vēma!

If he were to inspect his own horoscope,
With astrology revealing both good and bad,
Would the Lord not foresee the path of his
own fate?
Viśvadā-Abhirāma, vinura, Vēma!

This poem explores the idea of divine knowledge and fate. It asks if a deity, knowing their own destiny through astrology, would act differently to avoid mishaps. It makes us wonder whether knowing the future changes anything or if some events are simply unavoidable.

41

అగ్ని బానమేసి యంబుధి నింకించు

రాముడవలి కేగ రాక, నిలిచి

చెట్లు గిరులు తెచ్చి సేతువు గట్టడా

విశ్వదాభిరామ వినుర వేమ!

Agnibānamēsi yambudhi niṅkiñcu

Rāmuḍavali kēga rāka, nilici

Ceṭlu girulu tecci sētuvu gaṭṭaḍā

Viśvadābhirāma vinura, Vēma!

With the arrow of fire, he dried the ocean's waters,

Rāma stood steadfast once his course was set.

Did he not bring trees and hills to bridge the mighty sea?

Viśvadā-Abhirāma, vinura, Vēma!

42

స్త్రీ నెత్తిన రుద్రునకును
స్త్రీనోటను బ్రహ్మకెపుడు సిరిగుల్కంగా
స్త్రీ నెదిరిరొమ్మున హరికిని
స్త్రీ వెడపగ గురుడ నీవే దేవరవేమా!

Sthree netthina rudhrunakunu
Sthreenotanu brahmakepudu sirigulkamgaa
Sthree nedhirirommuna harikini
Sthree vedapaga guruda neeve dhevara
Vēma!

A lady resides on Rudra's head,
A lady dwells eternally on Brahma's tongue.
A lady rests upon Vishnu's chest, bestowing
endless fortune.
Without a woman, only you stand as the
true master, Vēma!

Vēmana humorously points out that the Trinity—Brahma, Vishnu, and Shiva—each have a woman in their lives. Shiva carries Goddess Ganga on his head, Brahma has Goddess Saraswati on his tongue, and Vishnu holds Goddess Lakshmi on his chest. Yet, Vēmana remarks that he alone is free from any troubles caused by a woman in his life!

43

రాముడొకడుపుట్టి రవికుల మీడెర్చె

కురుపతి జనియించి కులముజెఱిచె

ఇలను బుణ్యపాప మీలాగు కాదొకో

విశ్వదాభిరామ వినురవేమ!

Rāmuḍokaḍuputṭi ravikula mīḍĕrce

Kurupati janiyiñci Kulamujerace

Ilanu buṇyapāpa mīlāgu kādokō

Viśvadābhirāma vinuravēma!

Rama's birth alone exalted the glory of the
Sun dynasty,

While Duryodhana's birth tarnished the Kuru
lineage.

Thus, virtue and sin manifest in this world.

Viśvadā-Abhirāma, vinura, Vēma!

44

మంట లోహమందు మ్రాకుల శిలలందు

పటములందు గోడప్రతిమలందు

తన్నుదెలియు కొఅకుదగులదా పరమాత్మ

విశ్వదాభిరామ వినుర వేమ!

Maṇṭa lōhamandu mrākula śilalandu

Paṭamulandu gōḍapratimalandu

Tannudeliyu koṟakudaguladā paramātma

Viśvadābhirāma vinura, vēma!

In fire, in metal, in trees and stones,

In picture frames, wall hangings, and
murals—

The Divine resides, so we realize him.

Viśvadā-Abhirāma, vinura, Vēma!

45

జన్నములను మరియు జన్నియల ననేక

ముల నొనర్చియున్న ఫలముకాన

రాక యుండు నీతి లేకున్న మాత్రాన

విశ్వదాభిరామ వినుర వేమ!

Jannamulanu mariyu janniyala nanēka

Mula nonarciyunna phalamukāna

Rāka yuṇḍu nīti lēkunna mātrāna

Viśvadābhirāma vinura, Vēma!

Despite countless rituals and fervent prayers,

The results remain empty and fruitless.

It is only due to the absence of ethics.

Viśvadā-Abhirāma, vinura, Vēma!

SECTION 4

INSPIRATION AND PHILOSOPHY

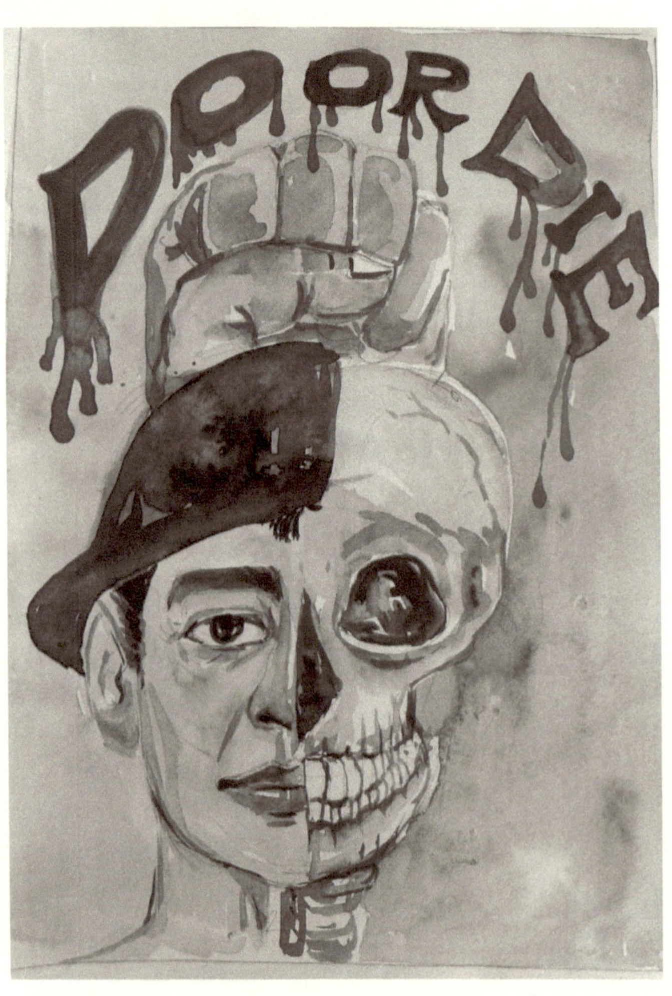

DO OR DIE

46

పట్టుపట్టరాదు పట్టి విడువరాదు

పట్టెనేని బిగియం బట్టవలెను

పట్టిడుడచుకన్న బడి చచ్చుటయెమేలు

విశ్వదాభిరామ వినుర వేమ!

Paṭṭupaṭṭarādu paṭṭi viḍuvarādu

Paṭṭenēni bigiyaṁ baṭṭavalenu

Paṭṭiḍuḍacukanna baḍi caccuṭayemēlu

Viśvadābhirāma vinura, Vēma!

Resolve firmly, let not waver.

Once resolved, seize it, grip it ever,

Rather fall and perish than buckle under!

Viśvadā-Abhirāma, vinura, Vēma!

47

రూపువంక పేరు రూఢిగా నిలుచును

పేరువంక క్రియలు పెనగుచుండు

నాశమౌను తుదకు నామరూప క్రియల్

విశ్వదాభిరామ వినుర వేమ!

Rūpuvaṅka pēru rūḍhigā nilucunu

Pēruvaṅka kriyalu penagucuṇḍu

Nāśamaunu tudaku nāmarūpa kriyal

Viśvadābhirāma vinura, Vēma!

Fame arises from beauty,

Deeds are achieved through fame.

Yet in the end, all—fame, beauty, and
deeds—fade to nothing.

Viśvadā-Abhirāma, vinura, Vēma!

48

లోభమోహములను ప్రాభవములు తప్ప

తలచిన పనులెల్ల తప్పి చనును

తానొకటి దలచిన దైవమొండగుచుండు

విశ్వదాభిరామ వినుర వేమ!

Lōbhamōhamulanu prābhavamulu tappu

Talacina panulella tappi canunu

Tānokaṭi dalacina daivamoṇḍagucuṇḍu

Viśvadābhirāma vinura, Vēma!

If one fails to grasp the weight of greed and
attachment,

All efforts will stray from their course.

He may plan for one path, but the divine will
lead another.

Viśvadā-Abhirāma, vinura, Vēma!

49

ఏవంక మనసు కలిగిన

నా వంకను నింద్రియంబులన్నియు నీగున్

నీవంక మనసు కల్గిన

ఏవంకకు నింద్రియంబు లేగవు వేమా!

Ēvaṅka manasu kaligina

Nā vaṅkanu nindriyambulanniyu nīgun

Nīvaṅka manasu kalgina

ēvaṅkaku nindriyambu lēgavu vēmā!

Where the mind takes root,

The senses are sure to flow.

When thoughts turn inward, they stay and
do not roam.

In such calm self-awareness, the senses find
their home, Vēma!

తన కుల గోత్రము లాకృతి

తన సంపద కలిమి బలిమి తనకేలనయా?

తన వెంటరావు నిజమిది

తన సత్యమే తోడువచ్చు తనతో

విశ్వదాభిరామ వినుర వేమ!

Tana kula gōtramu lākṛti
Tana sampada kalimi balimi tanakēlanayā?
Tana veṇṭarāvu nijamidi
Tana satyamē tōḍuvaccu tanatō
Viśvadābhirāma vinura vēma!

One's caste, lineage, and appearance,
Wealth, property, and power—of what use
are they to you?
None of these will follow you beyond this
life;
Only your truth will accompany you.
Viśvadā-Abhirāma, vinura, Vēma!

51

మనసే మాయా మృగమౌ
మననేమిటి పైకిగానీ మణిపోనీకా
మనసున మనసును జంపిన
మనందే ముక్తిగలదు మహిలో వేమ!

Manasē māyā mṛgamau
Mananēmiṭi paikigānī maṇipōnīkā
Manasuna manasunu jampina
Manandē muktigaladu mahilō vēma!

The mind becomes the illusory deer,
Questioning the purpose of life, unable to
relinquish life and desire.
If one can conquer the desires within the mind,
Liberation is found within, right here in this
world, Vēma!

In the Rāmāyaṇaṁ, the incident involving the golden deer, which is actually Maricha's illusion, illustrates a pivotal moment. Sita's desire to possess the enchanting deer prompts Lord Rāma to pursue it, leading him far from their abode. This sequence of events ultimately results in Sita's abduction by Ravana. Vēmana uses the metaphor of the illusory deer to reign in desires.

52

పండువలన బుట్టె బరగ ప్రపంచము
పండువలన బుట్టె పరము నిహము
పండు మేలెతీంగె బ్రహ్లోదుడిలలోన
విశ్వదాభిరామ వినుర వేమ!

Paṇḍuvalana buṭṭe baraga prapañcamu
Paṇḍuvalana buṭṭe paramu nihamu
Paṇḍu mēleṟiṅge brahlāduḍilalōna
Viśvadābhirāma vinura, vēma!

The world was born from the sacred 'fruit';
From it arise both life and the afterlife.
In this world, only Prahalada knew the true
essence of the FRUIT!
Viśvadā-Abhirāma, vinura, Vēma!

   * Prahalada, the son of the demon Hiranyakasipu,
recognized Vishnu as the Almighty from birth. He
understood that Vishnu exists in everything, as all
creation originates from the cosmic "fruit" and carries
its essence. This deep awareness set Prahalada apart,
showing his unwavering faith and divine wisdom.

53

భోగంటుల కాశింపక

రాగద్వేషంటు రంగుడదమలో

వేగమె మొక్ష పదంటును

రాగను నాతండు యొగిరాయుడు వేమ!

Bhōgambula kāśimpaka

Rāgadvēṣambu raṅguḍadamalō

Vēgame mōkṣa padambunu

Rāganu nātaṇḍu yōgirāyuḍu vēma!

Not seeking indulgences,

Suppressing likes and dislikes,

The one who strives for liberation early on

Is the finest among the wise, Vēma!

54

చనువారెల్లను జనులం

జనిపోయిన వారి పుణ్య సత్కథలెల్లన్

వినవలె గనవలె మనవలె

నని మషులకు దెలుసగూడ దంత్యము వేమ!

Canuvārellanu janulaṁ

Janipōyina vāri puṇya satkathalellan

Vinavale ganavale manavale

Nani maṣulaku delusagūḍa dantyamu vēma!

All men must face death;

The good deeds and stories of the departed,

We must listen, observe, and live by them.

Yet this truth dawns upon us only as we near the end, Vēma!

జనన మరణములన స్వప్న సుషుప్తులు
జగములందు నెండ జగములుండు
నరుడు జగమునంట నడుటాటు కాదొకో
విశ్వదాభిరామ వినుర వేమ!

Janana maraṇamulana svapna suṣuptulu
Jagamulandu neṇḍa jagamuluṇḍu
Naruḍu jagamunaṇṭa naḍubāṭu kādokō
Viśvadābhirāma vinura, Vēma!

Birth and death are but illusions, like dreams
in deep sleep;
In this realm, worlds abound, as countless
as the sun's rays.
Humans cannot grasp the entire vastness of
this cosmos.
Viśvadā-Abhirāma, vinura, Vēma!

56

 బ్రహ్మఘటము మేను ప్రాణంబు తగగాలి

మిత్రచంద్ర శిఖులు నేత్రచయము

మఱియు బ్రహ్మమనగ మహిమీద లేదయా

విశ్వదాభిరామ వినుర వేమ!

Brahmaghaṭamu mēnu prāṇambu tagagāli
Mitracandra śikhulu nētracayamu
Maṟiyu brahmamanaga mahimīda lēdayā
Viśvadābhirāma vinura, vēma!

Our body, a vessel crafted by Brahma, with
air as its vital breath;
The sun, the moon, and fire – the visible
elements of this realm.
Beyond these, no greater divine truth exists
in this world.
Viśvadā-Abhirāma, vinura, Vēma!

In Hinduism, Brahma is revered as the creator, shaping the universe and the body. The Sanskrit term *vayu*, meaning "wind" or "that which flows," represents the vital energy or life force. It regulates bodily functions and activities, sustaining life and connecting the physical and energy realms.

57

పగయుడగు గోపముడిగిన
పగయుడుగన్ కోర్కెలుడుగు
టరజన్మంపుం దగులుడుగు భేదముడిగిన
త్రిగుణము లుడుగంగ ముక్తి స్థిరమగు వేమ!

Pagayuḍagu gōpamuḍigina
Pagayuḍugan kōrkeluḍugu
Barajanmampuṁ daguluḍugu bhēdamuḍigina
Triguṇamu luḍugaṅga mukti sthiramagu
Vēma!

Reduce anger, and revenge will fade,
Lower grudges, and desires will wane,
Cease differences, and life bonds will sever
When the three gunas dissolve, only
steadfast salvation will remain, Vēma!

In Hindu philosophy, the concept of the Three *Gunas -Sattva, Rajas, and Tamas* - represents the fundamental qualities that influence human behaviour and the natural world. The interplay of these gunas influences our actions and mental states, and transcending them is seen as a path to achieving spiritual liberation and inner peace.

58

తామసించి చేయదగదెట్టి కార్యంటు

వేగిరింప నదియు విషమగును

పచ్చికాయదెచ్చి పడవేయ ఫలమౌనా?

విశ్వదాభిరామ వినుర వేమ!

Tāmasiñci cēyadagadeṭṭi kāryambu

Vēgirimpa nadiyu viṣamagunu

Paccikāyadecci paḍavēya phalamaunā?

Viśvadābhirāma vinura, Vēma!

No task should be done with careless neglect,

Haste turns even the sweetest work to poison.

Would ripening a raw vegetable make it a fruit?

Viśvadā-Abhirāma, vinura, Vēma!

59

చిత్తశుద్ధి కలిగిచేసిన పుణ్యంటు
కొంచెమైన నదియు కొదవగాదు
విత్తనంటు మర్రి వృక్షంటునకు నెంతో
విశ్వదాభిరామ వినుర వేమ!

Cittaśud'dhi kaligicēsina puṇyambu
Koñcemaina nadiyu kodavagādu
Vittanambu marri vṛkṣambunaku nentō
Viśvadābhirāma vinura, Vēma!

A good deed, however small, purifies the soul.
Though humble, it is never in vain.
Its worth is as grand as the seed of a mighty Banyan tree.
Viśvadā-Abhirāma, vinura, Vēma!

In the Indian context, a Banyan tree holds a special significance with religious and social importance. It represents longevity and grandeur through its propagation.

60

వినియు వినకయుండు కనియు గనక యుండు

తలచి తలపకుండు తాను యోగి

మనుజవరులచేత మణిపూజ గొనుచుండు

విశ్వదాభిరామ వినుర వేమ!

Viniyu vinakayuṇḍu kaniyu ganaka yuṇḍu

Talaci talapakuṇḍu tānu yōgi

Manujavarulacēta maṇipūja gonucuṇḍu

Viśvadābhirāma vinura, Vēma!

Hears but ignores, sees yet overlooks,

The one who contemplates without being swayed is a true Yogi.

Such a soul earns great respect and accolades from society.

Viśvadā-Abhirāma, vinura, Vēma!

శాంతమే జనులను జయమునొందించును

శాంతముననె గురువు జాడ తెలియు

శాంత భావ మహిమ జర్చింపలేమయా

విశ్వదాభిరామ వినుర వేమ!

Śāntamē janulanu jayamunondiñcunu

śāntamunane guruvu jāḍa teliyu

śānta bhāva mahima jarcimpalēmayā

Viśvadābhirāma vinura, Vēma!

Peace alone leads to victory for all,

Peace alone unveils the path to the Guru.

The glory of peace is beyond words to describe.

Viśvadā-Abhirāma, vinura, Vēma!

TIMELESS WISDOM & EVERYDAY INSIGHTS

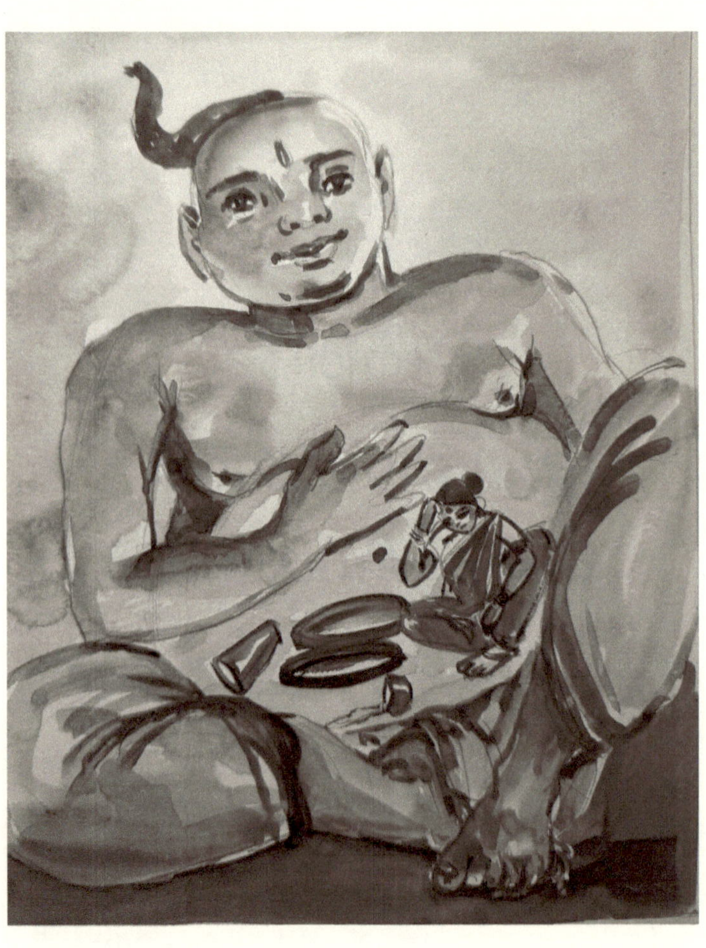

62

కల్లలాడువాని గ్రామకర్త యెఱుగు

సత్య మాడువాని స్వామి యెఱుగు

బెద్దతిండిపోతుం బెండ్లామెఱుంగురా

విశ్వదాభిరామ వినురవేమ!

Kallalāḍuvāni grāmakarta yeṟugu

Satya māḍuvāni svāmi yeṟugu

Beddatiṇḍipōtuṁ beṇḍlāmeṟuṅgurā

Viśvadābhirāma vinura,Vēma!

A village chief discerns the liar,

The Almighty knows the truthful,

And only the wife knows the glutton.

Viśvadā-Abhirāma, vinura, Vēma!

63

ఉప్పుకప్పురంటు నొక్క పోలికనుండు

చూడ జూడ రుచుల జాడవేరు

పురుషులందు పుణ్య పురుషులు వేరయా

విశ్వదాభిరామ వినురవేమా!

Uppukappurambu nokka pōlikanuṇḍu

Cūḍa jūḍa rucula jāḍavēru

Puruṣulandu puṇya puruṣulu vērayā

Viśvadābhirāma vinura, Vēmā!

Salt and camphor, in their appearance, may seem alike,

But only through tasting can one discern the difference, unlike.

Among men, thus, the virtuous shines, stands apart.

Viśvadā-Abhirāma, vinura, Vēma!

64

చంపదగినయట్టి శత్రువు తనచేత

జిక్కెనేని గీడు సేయరాదు

పొసగ మేలు చేసి పొమ్మనుటే చాలు

విశ్వదాభిరామ వినురవేమ!

Campadaginayaṭṭi śatruvu tanacēta

Jikkenēni gīḍu sēyarādu

Posaga mēlu cēsi pom'manuṭē cālu

Viśvadābhirāma vinura,Vēma!

If an enemy deserving death falls into your hands,

Harm him not.

Instead, doing good and letting him go is enough.

Viśvadā-Abhirāma, vinura, Vēma!

65

ఆపదగల వేళ అరసి బంధువు జూడు

భయము వేళ జూడు బంటుతనము

పేదవేళ జూడు పెండ్లాము గుణము

విశ్వదాభిరామ వినుర వేమ!

Āpadagala vēḷa arasi bandhuvu jūḍu

Bhayamu vēḷa jūḍu baṇṭutanamu

Pēdavēḷa jūḍu peṇḍlāmu guṇamu

Viśvadābhirāma vinura, Vēma!

In troubled times, observe your closest kin,

In fear, measure the courage within.

In poverty, uncover a wife's true nature.

Viśvadā-Abhirāma, vinura, Vēma!

66

అంతరంగమందు నపరాధములు చేసి

మంచి వానివలెనె మనుజుడుండు

ఇతరులెఱుగకున్న నీశ్వరుడెఱుగగడా?

విశ్వదాభిరామ వినురవేమ!

Antaraṅgamandu naparādhamulu cēsi

Mañci vānivalene manujuḍuṇḍu

Itarulerugakunna nīśvaruderugaḍā?

Viśvadābhirāma vinura,Vēma!

In the depths of his heart, he hides his sins,

Masquerading as a virtuous man.

Others may be deceived, but can the
Almighty be?

Viśvadā-Abhirāma, vinura, Vēma!

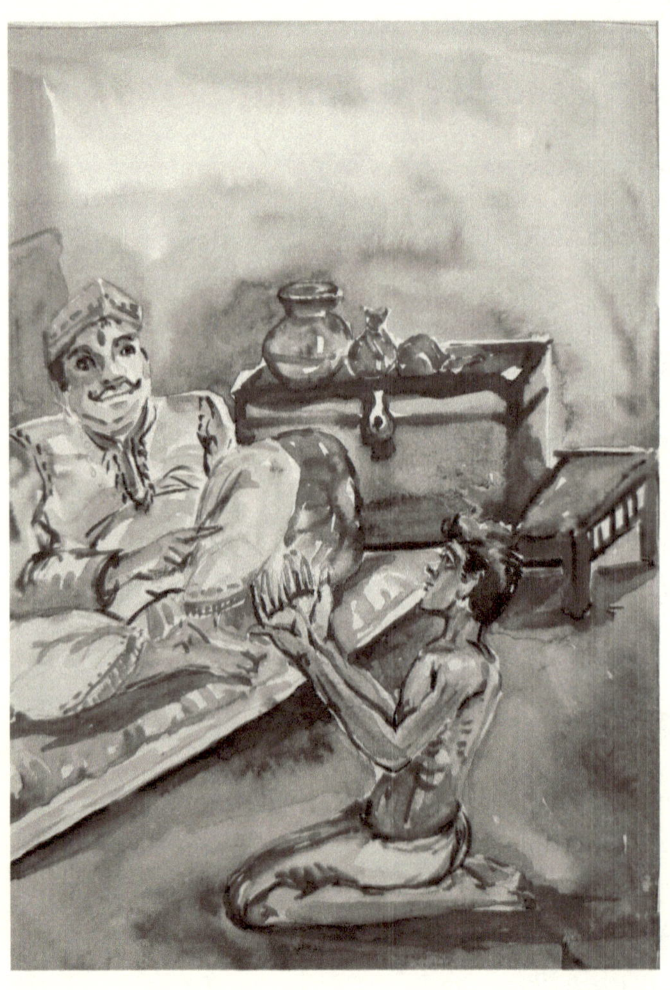

67

అడుగక ఆర్థమిచ్చు నతడు బ్రహ్మ జ్ఞాని

అడుగ నర్థమిచ్చునటడు త్యాగి

అడుగనీయలేని యాతడు పెను లోభి

విశ్వదాభిరామ వినురవేమ!

Aḍugaka ārdhamiccu nataḍu brahma jñāni

Aḍuga nardhamiccunaṭaḍu tyāgi

Aḍugaṇīyalēni yātaḍu penu lōbhi

Viśvadābhirāma vinura, Vēma!

The one who gives unasked is divinely wise,

The one who gives when asked is a generous giver.

But the one who withholds even when asked is a great miser!

Viśvadā-Abhirāma, vinura, Vēma!

A B C
D E F G
H I K L M
X O I O X I O I
O I X I O
X I O I O X I

బహుల కావ్యములను బరికింపగా వచ్చు
బహుల శబ్ద ఛాయం బలుకవచ్చు
సహనమొక్కోటబ్బా జాలా కష్టమ్ముదరా
విశ్వదాభిరామ వినురవేమ!

Bahula kāvyamulanu barikimpagā vaccu
Bahula śabdha chāyaṁ balukavaccu
Sahanamokkōṭabbā jālā kaṣṭamburā
Viśvadābhirāma vinura,Vēma!

Many literary texts may be dissected,
Countless words may be recited.
But patience, unmatched, is arduous.
Viśvadā-Abhirāma, vinura, Vēma!

అల్పుడెపుడు పల్కు నాడంతరముగాను

సజ్జనుండు బల్కు జల్లగాను

కంచుమ్రోగునట్లు కనకంబు మ్రోగునా

విశ్వదాభిరామ వినురవేమ!

Alpuḍepuḍu palku nāḍambaramugānu

Sajjanuṇḍu balku jallagānu

Kañcumrōgunaṭlu kanakambu mrōgunā

Viśvadābhirāma vinura, Vēma!

The lesser man boasts with pomp and pride,

The noble soul stands calm and dignified.

Does pure gold resound like clanging bronze?

Viśvadā-Abhirāma, vinura, Vēma!

70

తన విరక్తి యనెడి దాసి చేతను జిక్కి

మిగిలి పెడలవేక మిణుకుచున్న

నరుడి కేడముక్తి వరలెడి చెప్పడీ

విశ్వదాభిరామ వినుర వేమ!

Tana virakti yaneḍi dāsi cētanu jikki

Migili veḍalavēka miṇukucunna

Naruḍi kēḍamukti varaleḍi ceppaḍī

Viśvadābhirāma vinura, Vēma!

Bound by estrangement and bitterness,

Paralyzed, trapped, grappling in distress…

From whence can such a soul find salvation?

Viśvadā-Abhirāma, vinura, Vēma!

71

టీక వ్రాసినట్లనేకులు పెద్దలు

లోకమందు జెప్పి మంచు

కాకులట్టి జనుల కానరీ మర్మము

విశ్వదాభిరామ వినుర వేమ!

Ṭīka vrāsinaṭlanēkulu peddalu

Lōkamandu jeppi mañcu

Kākulaṭṭi janula kānarī marmamu

Viśvadābhirāma vinura, Vēma!

The wise and experienced have penned tales of wisdom,

Meant to enlighten and be shared with the world.

Yet men, like cawing crows, fail to grasp their hidden essence.

Viśvadā-Abhirāma, vinura, Vēma!

72

భయమంతయు దేహమునకె

భయ ముడిగిన నిశ్చయంటు పరమాత్మునకే

లయమంతయు జీవునకే

జయమాత్మకు ననుచు జగతిం జాటుర వేమ!

Bhayamantayu dēhamunake

Bhaya muḍigina niścayambu paramātmunakē

Layamantayu jīvunakē

Jayamātmaku nanucu jagatim jāṭura, Vēma!

All fear pertains to our bodies,

Choosing to transcend fear is godly.

Death claims only the living; the soul triumphs.

Proclaim it to the world, Vēma!

73

చదివి చదివి కొంత చదువంగ చదువంగ

చదువు చదివి యింకం జదువు చదివి

చదువు మర్మములను చదువలేడయ్యెను

విశ్వదాభిరామ వినుర వేమ.

Cadivi cadivi konta caduvaṅga caduvaṅga

Caduvu cadivi yiṅkam jaduvu cadivi

Caduvu marmamulanu caduvalēḍayyenu

Viśvadābhirāma vinura, Vēma!

Read and learn, then read and learn some more.

Study this, study that, and study even higher.

Yet fail to grasp the secret essence of true knowledge.

Viśvadā-Abhirāma, vinura, Vēma!

अतिथि देव भव

అతిథి రాక చూచి యదలించి పడవైచి
కఠిన చిత్తులగుచు గానలేరు
కర్మమునకు ముందు ధర్మము గానరో
విశ్వదాభిరామ వినుర వేమ!

Atithi rāka cūci yadaliñci paḍavaici
Kaṭhina cittūlagucu gānalēru
Karmamunaku mundu dharmamu gānarō
Viśvadābhirāma vinura, Vēma!

When an uninvited guest arrives, screaming
and sending them away,
The hard and callous-hearted fails to grasp
this truth.
Before actiing, reflect on the principles
upholding our society.
Viśvadā-Abhirāma, vinura, Vēma!

In Hinduism, *dharma* refers to principles and righteousness, while *karma* represents our actions. The teaching *Atithi Devo Bhava* means the uninvited guest is God. The poet beautifully intertwines *karma* and *dharma*, reminding us to think of *dharma* before we act (*karma*)."

75

అన్నిదానములను నన్న దానమే గొప్ప

కన్న తల్లికంటె ఘనములేదు

ఎన్న గురునికన్న నెక్కుడు లేడయా

విశ్వదాభిరామ వినురవేమ!

Annidānamulanu nanna dānamē goppa

Kannatallikaṇṭe ghanamulēdu

Ennagurunikanna nekkuḍu lēḍayā

Viśvadābhirāma vinura,Vēma!

Donating food, noblest charity's call,

A mother, the greatest gift of all.

Above your teacher, none stand tall.

Viśvadā-Abhirāma, vinura, Vēma!

76

తల్లితండ్రులందు దయలేని పుత్రుండు

పుట్టనేమి? వాడు గిట్టనేమి?

పుట్టలోని చెదలు పుట్టదా గిట్టదా

విశ్వదాభిరామ వినుర వేమ!

Tallitaṇḍrulandu dayalēni putruṇḍu

Puṭṭanēmi? Vāḍu giṭṭanēmi?

Puṭṭalōni cedalu puṭṭadā giṭṭadā?

Viśvadābhirāma vinura, Vēma!

A son devoid of love and care for his
parents,

What is the worth of his living? Or his end?

Like termites born and gone in their anthill
den.

Viśvadā-Abhirāma, vinura, Vēma!

77

జ్ఞానమెన్న గురువు జ్ఞానహైన్యము బుద్ధి

రెంటినందు రిమ్మ రేచునపుడు

రిమ్మ తెలిపెనేని రెండొక రూపురా

విశ్వదాభిరామ వినుర వేమ!

Ṅñānamenna guruvu ṅñānahain›yamu bud›dhi

Reṇṭinandu rim'marēcunapuḍu

Rim'ma telipenēni reṇḍoka rūpurā

Viśvadābhirāma vinura, Vēma!

Be it a wise sage or a thoughtless fool,

When composure is lost and idiosyncrasies emerge,

They appear no different from one another.

Viśvadā-Abhirāma, vinura, Vēma!

చదివి చదివి కర్మసారమ్ము గనలేక
తిరిగి తిరిగి తిరిగి దిమ్మరాయె
మరిగి తిరిగి మొరిగి మత్తిల్లి చచ్చెరా
విశ్వదాభిరామ వినుర వేమ!

Cadivi cadivi karmasāram'mu ganalēka
Tirigi tirigi tirigi dim'marāye
Marigi tirigi morigi mattilli caccerā
Viśvadābhirāma vinura, vēma!

Learn and learn, yet if you miss karma's core,
You'll wander and wander, and grow dim-witted more,
You'll stray, wander, criticise, drown, expire.
Viśvadā-Abhirāma, vinura, Vēma!

The context of *karma saaram* or meaning, here is from the Bhagavad Gita, in which Lord Krishna teaches that *karma* is essential to life, urging us to act selflessly and without attachment to outcomes.

ఆత్మబుద్ధి వలన నఖిలంబ తానయ్యె

జీవబుద్ధి వలన జీవుడయ్యె

మోహబుద్ధిలయము ముందర గనుగొను

విశ్వదాభిరామ వినుర వేమ!

Ātmabud›dhi valana nakhilamba tānayye

Jīvabud'dhi valana jīvuḍayye

Mōhabud'dhilayamu mundara ganugonu

Viśvadābhirāma vinura, vēma!

By knowing the soul's essence, one merges with the whole,

By understanding life's essence, one begins to truly live.

It's only at the brink of death that one sees the nature of desire.

Viśvadā-Abhirāma, vinura, Vēma!

తోపునిచ్చువాడు తోడనే నెరదాత

దోచుకున్ననాగు ద్రోహియయ్యె

ప్రాపు జూపువాడు పరమపుణ్యంబుడయ్యె

ప్రాపు చెరపువాడు పశువు వేమా!

Tōpuniccuvāḍu tōḍanē neradāta

Dōcukunnanāgu drōhiyayye

Prāpu jūpuvāḍu paramapuṇyumbuḍayye

Prāpu cerapuvāḍu paśuvu Vēmā!

The one who helps earns a place in our
hearts as a true giver.
The one who steals is marked as an enemy.
The one who grants a lifetime opportunity is
the most virtuous,
While the one who takes it away is a
monster, Vēma!

అప్పు లేని వాడు అధిక సంపన్నుడు

తప్పునేని వాడు ధరణి లేరు

గొప్ప లేని బుద్ధి కొంచెమై పోవురా

విశ్వదాభిరామ వినురవేమ!

Appu lēni vāḍu adhika sampannuḍu

Tappunēni vāḍu dharaṇi lēru

Goppa lēni bud'dhi koñcemai pōvurā

Viśvadābhirāma vinura,Vēma!

A debt-free man is truly rich, indeed,

A flawless one on Earth is rare to heed.

Shed pride, you won't be lessened!

Viśvadā-Abhirāma, vinura, Vēma!

82

కనులు పోవువాడు కాళ్లు పోయినవాడు

ఉభయులరయుగూడి యుండినట్లు

పేద పేద గూడి పెనగొని యుండును

విశ్వదాభిరామా వినుర వేమ!

Kanulu pōvuvāḍu kāḷlu pōyinavāḍu

Ubhayularayugūḍi yuṇḍinaṭlu

Pēda pēda gūḍi penagoni yuṇḍunu

Viśvadābhirāmā vinura vēma!

The blind and the sightless, both share their way,

The poor and the destitute, together they stay,

United in their plight, come what may.

Viśvadā-Abhirāma, vinura, Vēma!

83

వేషభాష లెరిగి కాషయవస్త్రముల్
గట్టగానె ముక్తి గలుగబోదు
తలలు బోడులైన తలపులు బోడులా
విశ్వదాభిరామ వినుర వేమ!

Vēṣabhāṣa lerigi kāṣayavastramul
Gaṭṭagāne mukti galugabōdu
Talalu bōḍulaina talapulu bōḍulā
Viśvadābhirāma vinura vēma!

By wearing the guise of saffron robes
And speaking the language of asceticism,
salvation is not attained.
Heads may be shaven and clean, but are
the thoughts truly pure?
Viśvadā-Abhirāma, vinura, Vēma!

Saffron robes, shaved heads, and ceremonial language symbolize renunciation and spiritual pursuit in many traditions. However, they serve as outward symbols and do not guarantee inner purity or true salvation.

84

గుణములోఁగలవాని కులమెంచగానేల
గుణము కలిగెనేని కోటిసేయు
గణములేక యున్న గుడ్డిగవ్వయులేదు
విశ్వదాభిరామ వినుర వేమ!

Guṇamulōgalavāni kulameñcagānēla
Guṇamu kaligenēni kōṭisēyu
Gaṇamulēka yunna guḍḍigavvayulēdu
Viśvadābhirāma vinura, Vēma!

Why point a finger at the origins of a person
with virtues?
With good qualities and virtues, one can
create wealth in crores.
There isn't a single cowrie, no matter its
flaws, that doesn't hold value.
Viśvadā-Abhirāma, vinura, Vēma!

Cowrie shells have held significant cultural, economic, and ornamental value. The term "cowrie" derives from the Hindi *kaudi*, which comes from Sanskrit *kaparda*. While smooth, shiny, and intact cowries were considered currency and valued, some not so perfect ones had their own value.

85

తప్పు లెన్నువారు తండోప తండంబు

లుర్వి జనులకెల్ల నుండు తప్పు

తప్పు లెన్నువారు తమ తప్పులెరుగరు

విశ్వదాభిరామ వినుర వేమ!

Tappu lennuvāru taṇḍōpa taṇḍambu

Lurvi janulakella nuṇḍu tappu

Tappu lennuvāru tama tappulerugaru

Viśvadābhirāma Vinura, Vēma!

Fault-finders are plentiful, a dime a dozen,

Flaws exist in all beneath the sun.

Those quick to judge others fail to see their own.

Viśvadā-Abhirāma, vinura, Vēma!

86

మాటజెప్ప వినని మనుజుడు మూర్ఖుడు

మాట విన్న నరుడు మానుడగును

మాట వినగ జెప్ప మానుట కూడదు

విశ్వదాభిరామ వినుర వేమ!

Māṭajeppa vinani manujuḍu mūrkhuḍu

Māṭa vinna naruḍu mānuḍagunu

Māṭa vinaga jeppa mānuṭa kūḍadu

Viśvadābhirāma vinura, Vēma!

A man who ignores what's spoken remains a fool,

One who listens with care earns respect and honour.

If your words are heard and valued, never cease to speak.

Viśvadā-Abhirāma, vinura, Vēma!

87

మాటలాడ వచ్చు మనసు నిల్వగలేదు

తెలుపవచ్చు దన్ను తెలియలేదు

సురియబట్టవచ్చు శూరుడు కాలేడు

విశ్వదాభిరామ వినుర వేమ!

Māṭalāḍa vaccu manasu nilvagalēdu

Telupavaccu dannu teliyalēdu

Suriyabaṭṭavaccu śūruḍu kālēḍu

Viśvadābhirāma vinura, Vēma!

One may speak with countless assurances, yet harbour a wavering mind.

One may inform and instruct, yet grasp not the depth within.

One may wield a sword with skill, yet fail to be a true warrior.

Viśvadā-Abhirāma, vinura, Vēma!

88

ఇంగలంబు తోడ నిల సల్పుతోడను

పరుని యాలితోడ పతితుతోడ

సరసమాడుటెల్ల చావుకు మూలము

విశ్వదాభిరామ వినుర వేమ!

Iṅgalambu tōḍa nila salputōḍanu

Paruni yālitōḍa patitutōḍa

Sarasamāḍuṭella cāvuku mūlamu

Viśvadābhirāma vinura, Vēma!

Toying with the embers of coal, courting
trouble,

Flirting with another's wife or befriending a
sinner,

Is the root cause of doom.

Viśvadā-Abhirāma, vinura, Vēma!

89

నడుచునిచ్చు నతని బత్తెమిచ్చిన వాని
కడుపు చల్లజేసి ఘనత విడుచు
నడుప నేర నేర నతడు నాలి ముచ్చేగదా?
విశ్వదాభిరామ వినుర వేమ!

Naḍucuniccu natani battemiccina vāni
Kaḍupu callajēsi ghanata viḍucu
Naḍupa nēra nēra nataḍu nāli muccēgadā?
Viśvadābhirāma vinura, Vēma!

The one who provides enough to sustain,
And satiates hunger, shows true largesse.
But the one who withholds even the bare
minimum – isn't he a thief?
Viśvadā-Abhirāma, vinura, Vēma!

90

మాటలాడు గల్గు మర్మములెరిగిన

పిన్నపెద్దతనము లెన్నవలదు

పిన్నచేతి దివ్వె పెద్దగా వెలగదా?

విశ్వధాభిరామ వినుర వేమ!

Māṭalāḍu galgu marmamulerigina

Pinnapeddatanamu lennavaladu

Pinnacēti divve peddagā velagadā?

Viśvadhābhirāma vinura vēma!

Those who speak wisely and grasp the
mysteries,

Shouldn't be judged by their age.

Isn't a lamp bright and radiant even when
held by the young?

Viśvadā-Abhirāma, vinura, Vēma!

పనసతోనలకన్న పంచదారలకన్న
జంటితేనెకన్న జున్నుకన్న
చెఱుకు రసముకన్న చెలుల మాటలె తీపి
విశ్వదాభిరామ వినుర వేమ!

Panasatonalakanna pañcadāralakanna
Juṇṭitēnekanna junnukanna
Ceṟuku rasamukanna celula māṭale tīpi
Viśvadābhirāma, vinura, Vēma!

Sweet as jackfruit, sweeter than sugar,
Honey from the comb, or custard,
Sweeter than sugarcane juice are the
beloved's words.
Viśvadā-Abhirāma, vinura, Vēma!

The poet uses the word *junnu*, a delicacy made from the colostrum-rich milk of a newly delivered cow, known for its unique sweetness and custard-like texture. There isn't an exact equivalent in English, but it is a cherished treat in many Indian households.

పదుగురాడుమాట పాడియై ధరజెల్లు
నొక్కడాడుమాట యెక్కదెందు
వూరకుండు వాని కూరెల్ల నోపదు
విశ్వదాభిరామ వినుర వేమ!

Padugurāḍumāṭa pāḍiyai dharajellu
Nokkaḍāḍumāṭa yekkadendu
Vūrakuṇḍu vāni kūrella nōpadu
Viśvadābhirāma vinura, vēma!

The world deems it fair when ten voices agree,
But a lone voice is seen as inadequate.
None can surpass the wisdom of the completely silent one.
Viśvadā-Abhirāma, vinura, Vēma!

This verse highlights the power of consensus, as many agreeing voices are valued over one. However, it emphasizes that true wisdom lies in silence, which transcends the need for validation or debate.

Prasanna Vedula Peri

తొత్తుతోటి పొందు తొట్టి పెసలమూట

ముచ్చతోటి పొందు తెచ్చుడి నింద

తలవదకపొందు తలతో దీరురా!

విశ్వదాభిరామ వినుర వేమ!

Tottutōṭi pondu toṟṟi pesalamūṭa

Mruccutōṭi pondu teccuḍi ninda

Talavadakapondu talatō dīrurā!

Viśvadābhirāma, vinura, Vēma!

Friendship with a good-for-nothing is like lentils in a torn sack,

Friendship with a thief brings nothing but disgrace.

Friendship with a fool ends with your head rolling!

Viśvadā-Abhirāma, vinura, Vēma!

తను వలచిన దావలచును తను

వలవక యున్ననెనడు తావలవ డిలన్

తనదు పటాటోపంబులు తన

మాయలు పనికిరావు ధరలోన వేమ!

Tanu valacina dāvalacunu tanu

Valavaka yunnanenaḍu tāvalava ḍilan

Tanadu paṭāṭōpambulu tana

Māyalu panikirāvu dharalōna Vēma!

If he desires her, she too will desire him,

If he remains indifferent, she will never seek him.

His baggage, his personal drama,

His sham and pretense, won't work in this world, Vēma!

95

 భూమి నాది యనిన భూమి ఫక్కున నవ్వు

దాన హీను జూచి ధనము నవ్వ

కదన భీతు జూచి కాలుండు నవ్వును

విశ్వదాభిరామ వినురవేమ!

Bhūmi nādi yanina bhūmi phakkuna navvu
Dāna hīnum jūci dhanamu navvu
Kadana bhītum jūci Kāluṇḍu navvunu
Viśvadābhirāma vinuravēma!

Claim the land as yours, and it will laugh
aloud in jest,
Money mocks the miser who hoards,
refusing to part,
In battle, Lord Yama chuckles at the
coward's fear.
Viśvadā-Abhirāma, vinura, Vēma!

Lord Yama, also known as *Kalamudu* (the Lord of
Time and Death), is the deity who governs death and
the afterlife in Hindu beliefs. He ensures the balance of
justice in life and thereafter.

96

కలిమిగల్గనేమి కరుణ లేకుండిన

కలిమి తగునె దుష్టకర్ములకును

తేనెగూర్పనీగ తెరువున బోవదా

విశ్వదాభిరామ వినుర వేమ!

Kalimigalganēmi karuṇa lēkuṇḍina

Kalimi tagune duṣṭakarmulakunu

Tēnegūrpanīga teruvuna bōvadā

Viśvadābhirāma vinura vēma!

What is the worth of riches without compassion?

What value is wealth in the hands of the wicked?

Does all the honey not go to the finder who passes by?

Viśvadā-Abhirāma, vinura, Vēma!

97

తప్పు పలుకు పలికి తాతోట చేసిన

కూడియున లక్ష్మీ క్రుంగిపోవు

నోటికుండ నీళ్ళు నొనరగా నిలుచునా

విశ్వదాభిరామ వినుర వేమ!

Tappu paluku paliki tātōṭa cēsina

Kūḍiyuna lakṣmī kruṅgipōvu

Nōṭikuṇḍa nīḷḷu nonaragā nilucunā?

Viśvadābhirāma vinura, Vēma!

With lies and deceit, wealth may grow,

But soon it will dwindle, ebb, and go.

Can water stay in your mouth-pot forever?

Viśvadā-Abhirāma, vinura, Vēma!

98

దశగలారినెల్ల దమ బంధువు లటండ్రు

దశయలేమి నెంత్రు తక్కువగను

దశయన గమ ధన దశమొక్కటే దశ

విశ్వదాభిరామ వినుర వేమ!

Daśagalārinella dama bandhuvu laṭaṇḍru

Daśayalēmi nentru takkuvaganu

Daśayana gama dhana daśamokkaṭē daśa

Viśvadābhirāma vinura vēma!

In good times, everyone claims to be your kin;

In hardship, you're dismissed and treated as less;

Come to think of it, wealth is the only true good time!

Viśvadā-Abhirāma, vinura, Vēma!

99

పరుల దత్తమొప్పి పాలనచేసిన

నిల స్వదత్తమునకు విను మడియగు

నవని పరుల దత్త మహాపరింపగ రాదు

విశ్వధాబిరామ వినుర వేమ!

Parula dattamoppi pālanacēsina
Nila svadattamunaku vinu maḍiyagu
Navani parula datta mahaparimpaga rādu
Viśvadhābirāma vinura, Vēma!

Accept with devotion what others freely give,
Govern it wisely, with care and grace.
Land that is donated must never be usurped.
Viśvadā-Abhirāma, vinura, Vēma!

This poem reflects the milieu of kings and landlords, where land was often donated as a gesture of generosity and devotion. It emphasizes the ethical duty to govern such gifts wisely and never to usurp it.

100

తల్లీ బిడ్డలకు తగవు పుట్టించెడి

ధనము సుఖము గూర్చనని గడింత్రు

కానీయెల్ల యెడల ఘన దుఃఖకరమది

విశ్వదాభిరామ వినుర వేమ!

Tallī biḍḍalaku tagavu puṭṭiñceḍi

Dhanamu sukhamu gūrcunani gaḍintru

Kānīyella yeḍala ghana duḥkhakaramadi

Viśvadābhirāma vinura, Vēma!

That which breeds discord between mother and child

Money - that is earned for the sake of happiness

But, in every instance, it is money that brings deep sorrow.

Viśvadā-Abhirāma, vinura, Vēma!

101

కుండ కుంభమన్న కొండ పర్వతమన్న
నుప్పు లవణమన్న నోకటి కాదె
భాష లిట్టె వేరు పరతత్త్వమొకటి
విశ్వదాభిరామ వినుర వేమ!

Kuṇḍa kumbhamanna koṇḍa parvatamanna
Nuppu lavaṇamanna nokaṭi kāde
Bhāṣa liṭṭe vēru paratattvamokaṭe
Viśvadābhirāma vinura vēma!

Be it a pot or a cauldron, a hill or a mount,
Sea salt or salt - are they not the same?
Words may differ, yet the essence stays
true.
Viśvadā-Abhirāma, vinura, Vēma!

This poem serves as an epilogue, reflecting the spirit of the entire book. While the words I've chosen in translation may differ, my hope is that they capture the true essence and soul of Vēmana's timeless wisdom.

Acknowledgements

This work would not have been possible without the help, advice and contributions from several people in the last two years as I embarked on this project. A special callout to two of them.

Saripalli Lakshmi, dedicated school teacher and scholar of Telugu literature, who guided me through Vēmana's *padyalu* and helped me preserve their essence in English. She tirelessly responded to my messages and queries at odd hours and with utmost patience, and was the first to encourage my endeavour in this subject.

Dipanwita Halder, whose surrealistic illustrations have infused this work with vibrant life, connecting words and art in a mesmerizing symphony.

Other Gems To Refer To

Brown, CP. 2003. *Verses of Vēmana.* New Delhi, Chennai: Asian Educational Services.

Narla, V. R. 1969. *Makers of Indian Literature - Vēmana.* SAHITYA AKADEMI, New Delhi.

Patil, Mallikarjun. 2018. *Mahayogi Vēmana.* Dharwad: Mahayogi Vēmana Peetha Karnatak University.

Madhuranthakam, Narendra, Gurram Bhanumurthy. 2017. *VĒMANA.* Tirupati: Tirumala Tirupati Devasthanams.

https://slokam.in/Vēmana-satakam-in-english-Vēmana-padyalu/.

https://telugucorner.com/Vēmana.php.

https://vignanam.org/english/Vēmana-satakam.html.

https://www.andhrabharati.com/shatakamulu/Vēmana/index.html.

https://desibantu.com/.

https://mahayogiVēmanapeetha.in/Books.html.

Early Impressions

"'Hundred and One verses of Vēmana' is more than just an incredible introduction to an insightful poet, but a work so richly textured and carefully crafted that it feels like a conversation with the wise sage himself. This clear and approachable translation is a must-read for those seeking to discover and connect with Telegu heritage, philosophy and art." **Mruthyunjay Rao K (Canada based Writer for Films and TV)**

========================

"Vemana's words, a mystic's sight,

Translated now, a wondrous light.

From Telugu's depths, a treasure's birth,

Shared with the world, of immense worth

Vemana Satakam, originally written in Telugu, is a timeless collection of aphorisms and moral verses. A masterful translation of this classic into English has brought its wisdom to a new audience. Prasanna Garu skillfully retains the original's lyrical beauty, simplicity, and profound messages about life, ethics, and spirituality. This work bridges traditional and contemporary readers, ensuring Vemana's legacy endures." **Rajesh Toleti, UK based literary enthusiast, Cambridge Examination Board member, and Software Architect.**

============================

"Vēmana, celebrated as the 'People's Poet,' has inspired generations with his poems. This book continues his tradition, adapting his wisdom for modern society while promoting the rich contributions of Telugu language. By translating these works into English, Prasanna bridges cultures, inviting both Telugu speakers and English readers to connect with Vēmana's timeless legacy." **Saripalli Lakshmi, Triple MA (Telugu, Sanskrit, and History), is a dedicated Telugu teacher, and a passionate literary enthusiast.**